GLORY DAYS

Transport in Liverpool

Adrian Jarvis

Ian Allan PUBLISHING

Title page:
Liverpool Overhead Railway Set 41 2-4-2 approaching Gladstone Dock station in 1953. Sets 41-2-42 came from the last batch of new (as distinct from rebuilt) stock, dating from as recently as 1895.
P. B. Whitehouse / Colour-Rail IR431

Front cover:
A summer's day at the bottom of Water Street, in the shadow of the Cunard Building. No trams, sadly — just lots of shiny new buses — but the Overhead provides us with some original stock northbound (ie heading towards picture left) and some rebuilt stock headed south. Some classic cars here too, including a Vauxhall Wyvern/Velox (c1955) and a Humber Hawk. Notice the Scammell Scarab in the background, doubtless headed for the BRS depot at Manchester Dock.
T. J. Edgington / Colour-Rail IR61

Back cover:
'De Float'n' Chippy' — *Royal Iris* if you wish to be formal — approaching the floating stage during an evening cruise towards the end of her career. (Notice the MPTE logo on her starboard exhaust pipe — er, sorry... stack.) Pretty she undoubtedly was not, and yet there's no doubt she was one of the icons of the glory days.
John Ryan

Contents

First published 2001

ISBN 0 7110 2735 8

Published by Ian Allan Publishing

an imprint of Ian Allan Publishing Ltd, Hersham, Surrey KT12 4RG.
Printed by Ian Allan Printing Ltd, Hersham, Surrey KT12 4RG.

Code: 0105/B2

Acknowledgements

Writing this book was a spare-time project which has been bedevilled with family and other problems which have placed me under pressure in various ways and made the whole thing take far too long. When you are working late at night, writing words is easier than finding pictures, and I should like to thank my old friend John Ryan for helping me with many illustrations from his very large collection, and Roy Forshaw, another fellow-member of the Merseyside Industrial Heritage Society, for some more. Everyone at Ian Allan, but particularly Peter Waller, Nick Grant and Paul Cripps, has been very patient and they too helped me enormously with finding illustrations. I do not think it inappropriate to mention Cheshire County Libraries, whose Widnes Library has an excellent room dedicated to public transport, which provides almost everything one needs within a relatively small space. I spent a few useful Saturday mornings there, and promise not to refer to Widnesians as 'woollybacks' ever again. Well, not for a while, anyway.

I know it's a cliché to thank one's partner, but my wife Anthea really did show great forbearance in tolerating my being in the library when I should have been shopping, or in the study when it was my turn to cook.

Like many of my colleagues in National Museums & Galleries on Merseyside, I have benefited from the 'home loan' of an obsolescent PC, which saved me from spending a lot of money on a machine I wouldn't understand when all I needed was a high-tech typewriter.

Adrian Jarvis
Liverpool
January 2001

Introduction

So far back as we can trace Liverpool's history, the town made its money from the river and the sea. In the 18th century it became, and it remains, a major international port, still making its money from moving things around. But being a port means much more than handling international cargo vessels: goods must come from inland for export and imports must be forwarded inland. Furthermore, both the vessels and the cargoes belong to people, and in the days before cheap and effective telecommunications were available, the business of a port could only be done by people travelling to meet each other and close their deals. Even in these days of e-mail and tele-conferencing, some business is better done in person anyway — including the preliminary discussions of the form this book would take.

The result was that Liverpool, like any other great port city, developed a network of coastal and inland communications to serve its 'glamour' trades from an early stage — indeed, in several cases, from a pioneering stage. The first industrial canal (the Sankey Navigation), the first English canal to run independently of a river valley (the Bridgewater Canal) and the first English canal to cross a watershed (the Trent & Mersey) were all financed and used by customers of the port of Liverpool. The first modern railway (defined as all steam-hauled and all double-track) was financed from Liverpool to run to Manchester. The communications role of the port was emphasised by its being the terminal for the first contracted transatlantic mails carried by steam, introduced by Cunard in 1840, but in fact the Liverpool & Manchester Railway had initially made most of its money from passengers — ie from business communications — rather than from freight.

The mention of Cunard calls to mind Liverpool's role in the development of the 'Atlantic Ferry'. If Bristol provided the starting point and Glasgow much of the technical expertise, it was Liverpool, with its superior commercial know-how and, critically, its skills in directing and financing the work of its dock engineers, that dominated the route. During the 'reign' of Jesse Hartley as Dock Surveyor (ie Chief Engineer), 1824-60, the Liverpool Dock Trustees became the largest and most successful single port authority in the world. Two large dock-building programmes, completed respectively in 1847 and 1848 at a cost of over £2,000,000, would have been the cue in most ports for a period of consolidation and paying off some of the debts. Liverpool went for growth: having defeated every rival except London the Dock Trustees now sought completely to outdistance them by building yet more and bigger new docks.

Back in the mid-1820s, Liverpool had established an optical telegraph system extending from Anglesey to the town centre. A little earlier, the first regular steam ferries had started plying the Mersey; a little later the first iron vessels to be built locally slid into their natural element. Liverpool was never a shipbuilding centre to compete with Glasgow, but it had its moments, as when it excelled in building high-speed steel steamships for running the Yankee blockade during the American Civil War.

All these events and many others might suggest that Liverpool's glory days in terms of transport are to be found in the second third of the 19th century. By about 1860 Liverpool was showing some signs (albeit recognisable only with hindsight) of losing her pre-eminence. Other British ports began to catch up a little, and continental ports on great rivers benefited from the traffics of the huge hinterlands they could serve via the Rhine or the Elbe. Late in the century, Liverpool was home to *Campania* and *Lucania*, which were followed in 1907 by *Mauretania* and *Lusitania*, probably the greatest transatlantic greyhounds of them all. Some of her great entrepreneurs, like Sir Alfred Jones or the Vestey brothers, both opened and dominated major new

trades or trading areas, yet while success was still commonplace, out-distancing was a thing of the past.

These, too, were glory days, but they are not the glory days with which this book is concerned either. You cannot buy an instrument known as a glory meter: glory is an entirely immeasurable and irrational 'thing'. It is not just immeasurable, defying the dour calculations of economists; it is altogether unreal. Glory, which is perhaps best explained in modern parlance as a 'feel-good factor', is a state of mind.

So when did Scousers feel glorious? One might answer that many of them are natural optimists who buy National Lottery tickets and therefore feel glorious most of the time, except when they have just discovered that they have not won. A slightly cooler judgement might be that, during the putative golden age suggested above, there was relatively little feeling of glory, because it was chiefly a small and rich minority who experienced it. One time we may be quite sure that only a minority felt glorious was during the so-called Edwardian Indian Summer,

which was in fact a very troubled period indeed, with severe sectarian strife on the streets supplemented by the transport and other strikes of 1911 which saw the city effectively under martial law. There is just one significant exception to this picture of Edwardian gloom, which is the use by John Brodie, City Engineer, of the electric tramcar as an instrument of slum clearance and social improvement by enabling the city to spread out, decreasing population density in the less desirable areas. But that was probably cancelled out by the decision of the White Star Line to move its express passenger liners to Southampton.

There was a brief boom after the Great War, but it soon collapsed, and that collapse saw Liverpool's port and industries struggling until the recovery of the late '30s, with a new record tonnage set in 1938. World War 2 hit Liverpool very hard: whilst nearly all the Luftwaffe attacks took place within a single week in May 1941, the damage done was enormous, and it has been argued that, in relation to area and population, Liverpool in fact

▲ This 1949 Leyland PD2/Roberts, L443, is standing at the top of Moorfields in 1964, waiting for passengers from Exchange station, just visible in the background. It was working a circular service connecting the stations with the floating stage for the 'IoM and North Wales Steamers'. And, of course, they *were* steamers. *Geoff Lumb*

5

The original James Street station was destroyed in the Blitz. This temporary building lasted into the late '60s and its replacement is unattractive, but what matters for our purposes is that the temporary building managed to shift the passengers, millions of them. One might also carpingly remark that its non-computerised destination indicators worked fairly well. *John Ryan*

Oil-seed milling was a major employer during the glory days, but oil-seed mills are now physically much smaller and much less labour-intensive. *Author*

suffered more damage than either London or Coventry. As in World War 1, Liverpool shipowners and merchants suffered very heavy losses to German U-boats and surface raiders; this time there were aircraft as well.

Yet these grim happenings were the threshold of what I am going to portray as the glory days. It is a slightly quirky view of glory, but it is rooted in the feel-good factor. In the years between about 1953 ('the dawn of the New Elizabethan Era', they called it at the time) and 1970, Liverpudlians had every reason to believe that they had kept most of the best of the past, that they were doing very nicely now, and that the good times were just beginning. They might not quite have believed Mr Macmillan's election slogan 'You've never had it so good', but they came close. As it happens, they were wrong, but glory, remember, is in the eye of the beholder.

Underpinning the whole business was the state of trade through the port, which improved steadily during the '50s and reached a new record level in 1964. A handful of insiders already knew of Sea-Land's pioneering efforts with containers, but anyone who had suggested in 1964, whether in a bar on the Dock Road or over a suburban dinner table, that the congested cargo-liner berths in Liverpool's South Docks, where ships were often berthed two or three abreast, would be closed in eight years' time would have been regarded as barking mad. Everyone could see, from the congestion on the Dock Road, how well the port was doing, and you did not need to be the 1960s' answer to Homer to know that when the port did well, the city did well.

Liverpool had long been a moderately important manufacturing centre. In the 18th century this had been based on such as salt, pottery, copper and whale-oil products. In the 19th there was a fair bit of mechanical engineering and large-scale processing of primary commodities like sugar, oil seeds and tobacco. It is a little-known fact that at the 1891 Census there were more shipbuilding workers in Liverpool than in Birkenhead, where the Cammell Laird yard was producing strings of famous ships. There were also more skilled metal-workers (aggregated for all trades) than in Manchester.

Between the wars some quite high-tech industries settled in and around Liverpool, including an important turbine factory, large-scale light engineering works and two major pharmaceutical manufacturers. By the 1960s these had been supplemented with a wide variety of production engineering facilities, most notably the Ford and British Leyland factories at Halewood and Speke, which attracted a considerable number of satellite firms supplying and servicing them. The food industry was also well represented, with large factories producing things like biscuits, jam and margarine which used the products of the local primary producers of flour, sugar or vegetable oils.

We now know that most of these had fatal or potentially fatal weaknesses. Many of them have gone, and those which survive have undergone periodic crises. This economic fragility is best illustrated by the case of dock labourers. In the record tonnage year of 1964 about 25,000 of them worked in the port; in 1999 a greater tonnage was shifted by under 400. But that is only the beginning of the change. Where now, in the age of the container and the bulk carrier, are the cratemakers, the sack-repairers, the coopers and the riggers? The tackle-makers, the tarpaulin-makers, the lifebelt-cover-makers, the ships' fender-makers and the ships' medicine-chest-replenishers? Gone, almost every man-jack of them. Even the pubs along the Dock Road have mostly closed: ships of 60,000dwt turn round literally in a day or two, and their relatively tiny crews do not even have time for the traditional 'run ashore'. Nor do the ships stay in Liverpool to use drydocks: of 13 which were in commission in 1964, three remain, including both of the two smallest. The majority of the scalers and painters have gone the way of the dock labourers. The Cammell Laird yard in Birkenhead is enjoying a great revival in ship conversion and major repair work, but the routine 'scale and paint' work is largely gone: it is cheaper to have it done in Southeast Asia where they are not so particular about the toxic nature of the scale left in the bottom of the drydock, to say nothing of that in the lungs of the workers.

Perched in the woods is the Eastham Ferry Hotel. The Eastham Ferry was for a short time the best route from Chester to Liverpool, then became 'The Richmond of the Mersey', handling mainly weekend pleasure traffic. But in the glory days Eastham was mooted as a hovercraft terminal. There were plenty of dafter suggestions made.
John Ryan

When all those tens of thousands of shipping-related workers were milling around there was a huge demand for trains, trams, buses, ferryboats. But they were by no means the whole story. At the end of the 19th century there were some 10,000 messenger-boys in the city, and while they dwindled rapidly in the face of telephone competition, there were still significant numbers of them in the late '50s. In the early 1960s British Railways' busiest station in terms of passengers per platform/yard/day was Liverpool James Street. Lots of people were moving around, not just commuting but also in the daily conduct of their business.

Then came the heady days when The Beatles ruled the charts and Liverpool and Everton ruled football. First Alan Rudkin, then John Conteh won world boxing championships in the days when there were just eight weights and one governing body, as distinct from today's situation where there are a hundred or so 'world champions' around. Liverpool comedians, whether of the older generation like Arthur Askey or the younger like Jimmy Tarbuck, were prominent, though the featherweight title then as now was held by Ken Dodd's tickling stick.

The average citizen knew little of exactly what the boffins in the University did, but some of them were aware that Liverpool scientists had played a significant

part in the theoretical lead-up to the development of the atom bomb, and some knew, if only through Parkinson's Law, of Liverpool's leading role in postwar particle physics. They knew that it was among the hardest universities to get into for Medicine or Veterinary Science. In other matters cultural, they knew that they had the biggest Anglican cathedral in the world, and the Roman Catholic Cathedral, rising on the skyline, could still be nicknamed 'Paddy's Wigwam' without the intervention of the Race Relations Board. The Liverpool Philharmonic Orchestra had, since 1957, been the *Royal* LPO — then the only Royal orchestra outside London. Some mean-minded souls noted that the Hallé Orchestra did not achieve this recognition. One area of transport history which remains to be researched is the social history of the urchins who collected protection money on your car when parking to go the 'The Phil' in the '60s, before the deteriorating housing in the area was re-gentrified. (Nowadays one is confronted instead with the sons of professors seeking sponsorship for a hike across the Darien Gap in aid of something fearfully 'PC' — the old system of giving the recognised 6d to a genuinely needy brat was probably preferable.) By 1957, the City Library and the City Museum were both reopened after serious bomb damage, as was the Great Hall of St George's Hall, so Liverpool could celebrate the 750th anniversary of its 'Charter' (strictly, Royal Letters Patent) with some grounds for optimism.

While all these successes were happening, and changes going on, the transport scene had suffered some serious losses. The Overhead Railway closed in 1956 and the trams, after a long run-down, finally went the following year. The Liverpool & North Wales steamers stopped in 1962. Yet these seemed no ground for despondency, merely a grudging acknowledgement that things change, for the other side of the coin was that the Mersey Railway had smart new trains, the Mersey Ferries had new boats, the Corporation was investing heavily in new rear-engined buses and the electrification of the main line to London was in hand. Across the river at Moreton, Merseyside could briefly boast the first public hovercraft

service in the country, across the mouth of the Dee estuary to Rhyl. It was admittedly experimental and ran only for the summer season of 1962, but hovercraft were, for a while, perceived as being at the cutting edge of a forthcoming transport revolution. If one were to believe the popular press of the day, everything from the *Queen Mary* through BP's tanker fleet to the rowing boats on Sefton Park lake would soon be replaced by hovercraft. Some of the proposals for their use were actually quite sensible, such as a link from central Liverpool to the Airport and the reinstatement of the old Eastham Ferry route, but none of them came to pass. Yet, anticipating the white heat of Harold Wilson's technological revolution, what seemed like an important new technology was being pioneered on Merseyside.

Another technological issue pursued with great enthusiasm by the local press was that of nuclear-propelled merchant ships. The American experimental vessel *Savannah* had been launched in 1959, and two years later she was sent on extended sea trials ballasted to her intended working draught; another two years after that she actually carried cargoes between Europe and the US. The hard-nosed hacks of *Lloyd's List* and the *Journal of Commerce* tried to inject some ingredient of economic commonsense into their reports, but the non-specialist press went completely haywire. Now the hovercraft on Sefton Park lake would do 60 knots by nuclear power at a cost of 0.001d/mile. It is a particularly difficult issue into which to 'think ourselves back': before it became common knowledge that so-called 'peaceful uses' of atomic power were nothing more than an adjunct to the arms industry and when the only significant nuclear accident (at Calder Hall) had been successfully kept secret, the idea of a merchant ship which could do a year's work at a speed of 30 knots for the use of less than a hundredweight of fuel seemed a miracle of technology from which we must all benefit.

It was, of course, a load of nonsense: nuclear power was totally uneconomic and would only be successfully applied to warships. Only one further merchant vessel was built, but it seemed at first like a great new era in

merchant shipping, and from the enthusiasm with which it was reported arose the feeling that it would be a technological new dawn for Liverpool. We knew, after all, how our forebears had profited from the sucession of new technologies they had adopted.

Nobody at the time knew that the Mersey Ferries' new boats would still be in service in 2000 except for the famous 'Float'n' Chippy', known to Lloyd's Register as the *Royal Iris,* which was sold off as beyond economic repair. Nor did they know that a handful of Atlanteans with letter *suffixes* would still be on the road then, driving around in clouds of variously black and blue smoke. They didn't know that Exchange station would be shut, so that, for purposes of going to Scotland, Liverpool would be on a branch line from Wigan. They didn't know that their new 100mph service to London would be slower in 2000 than it was 1970. Perhaps above all they failed to realise the imminent disaster looming through the overspill policies implemented by the City Council of the day — policies which were, as elsewhere, largely responsible for 'the inner cities problem'. Finally, they largely failed to recognise the extremely low quality of most of the new buildings of the '60s, which have aged so ungracefully as truly to deserve the cliché 'concrete deserts', and more than a few conspicuously bad examples have already been demolished.

But of the ordinary Liverpudlians of the '60s, among whom I was an undergraduate, it could fairly be said that, in their ignorance, they enjoyed their glory days.

Ferries

Cities on major estuaries need convenient means of crossing them, as witness the multiple bridges of Newcastle, London or Glasgow. The Mersey was rather wider, and was bedevilled with people who wanted enough clearance under any proposed bridge to be able to sail (very) tall ships under it, unladen and on a high equinoctial spring tide. In the early 1860s, the Mersey

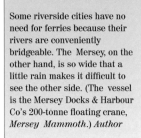

Some riverside cities have no need for ferries because their rivers are conveniently bridgeable. The Mersey, on the other hand, is so wide that a little rain makes it difficult to see the other side. (The vessel is the Mersey Docks & Harbour Co's 200-tonne floating crane, *Mersey Mammoth*.) *Author*

Docks & Harbour Board considered a scheme for an overhead telegraph cable across the Mersey and assumed the necessity of a minimum clearance of 160ft![1] The legacy is that there is still no Mersey Bridge downstream of Runcorn, though there have been many proposals. As a result, ferries for the carriage of both passengers and goods were not just important but a crucial part of the Liverpool transport scene from medieval times until 1934, when the first Mersey road-tunnel was opened.

Over the centuries there had been many ferry undertakings on the Mersey, their Wirral landing-points spread from New Brighton to Runcorn, but those upstream of Eastham (ie to Ellesmere Port and Runcorn) existed principally to connect with horse-drawn canal packet-boats and are not normally considered part of the ancestry of the modern Mersey Ferries. The welter of small companies gradually resolved themselves into larger units, and ultimately, by merger or closure, into just two, namely the municipal undertakings of Birkenhead and Wallasey. Wallasey Local Government Board had run ferries since 1862, while the Birkenhead Improvement Commissioners had begun their services in 1842. Curiously, Liverpool took little interest in ferries, controlling only one fairly brief and unprofitable venture; all the important ones were financed and managed from the Wirral side of the river.

The first major threat the surviving ferry operators faced was from the Mersey Railway, initially proposed in 1866 and opened in 1886, but a railway which was steam-hauled in deep tunnel was a comprehensively dirty and nasty experience, though it initially did the ferries some damage. Fortunately for the latter, it was also a financial shambles, largely because far too much of its cost had

---

[1] Underwater cables were, of course, in use by then, but the Board feared repeated problems with anchors and dredgers damaging a cable under the Mersey, hence the serious consideration of what seems at first sight like a lunatic idea.

The Mersey's big tidal range meant that at low water of spring tides the link-span bridges of the original stage were too steep for draught horses. This 'floating roadway' was introduced in 1874 to reduce the gradient, and continued in use until 1990. *Roy Forshaw*

An unusual view showing the floating roadway in left foreground with no queue to speak of to get on the luggage-boat, which is just finishing discharging. *John Ryan*

13

One place the glory days did not reach was the ferry terminus at Birkenhead (Woodside). This view dating from the early 1900s (there is a rank of 'growlers' in the background) was substantially unchanged apart from the substitution of buses for trams. *John Ryan*

▲

been met from debenture stocks and nowhere near enough from the issue of ordinary shares (which was also, of course, the main reason for the troubles of the Channel Tunnel, a century later). It went into receivership in 1887, largely as a result of the initiative of Birkenhead Council — a principal competitor for the cross-river trade. Blundering from crisis to crisis, the railway's already inadequate revenue declined steadily until electrification was completed in 1903. It was a financial miracle it survived that long, and, despite triumphalist announcements from both the Mersey Railway Company and British Westinghouse, the contractors for the conversion, it was then hit by severe technical teething troubles. When these were overcome, the railway threatened another potential crisis for the ferries, particularly the Birkenhead ones, but again they survived, through a combination of low fares and sensible connections with trams and buses on both sides of the river. As before, there was a serious initial drop in ferry passengers, followed by a slow but steady recovery. The Wallasey Ferries were less affected, because the Wirral Railway, connecting with the Mersey at Birkenhead Park, failed to serve some of the main 'dormitory' areas of the town. The critical question lay further ahead: whether the ferries generally, and the Birkenhead ones in particular, would be able to raise the money to modernise their ageing fleets of steamers after World War 2.

The opening of the road tunnel caused damage to the vehicle-carrying 'luggage boats' which was both immediate and critical, but not quite fatal because the road-tunnel was unsuitable for horse-drawn vehicles, the last handful of which survived until the early '60s. However, in 1941 the Woodside service ceased and the Seacombe one followed it in 1947. They had never been equal to the traffic and were probably only loved in retrospect by those who had not had to queue to get aboard them with a vehicle. The passenger ferries were a different matter.

A common sight in the glory days: one ferry (*Mountwood*) seen from another (*Royal Daffodil*). The ferries now run one 'triangular' route instead of two 'out and backs'.
John Ryan

The present *Royal Daffodil* (previously named *Overchurch*) drifts against wind and tide to come alongside the Liverpool floating stage. *Author*

After the war, both undertakings rose to the challenge with new motor vessels, Birkenhead with *Mountwood, Woodchurch* (in service 1960) and *Overchurch* (1962), and Wallasey with *Royal Iris* (III) launched in 1950, *Leasowe* (II) and *Egremont* (II)[2] in 1950/1. These were not the foolish gesture they might appear: they provided a quarter-hourly service which never really lost out to the trains; it was the cars, and especially the diminution in congestion for cars brought about by completion of the second road-tunnel in 1972, that chiefly harmed them. In the '50s and '60s they were heavily laden at rush hour, being especially favoured on the one hand by those with bicycles and motorcycles and on the other by those who preferred the fresh air and took part in one of Merseyside's odd little rituals — that of walking round and round the boat deck in single file throughout the crossing, always in an anti-clockwise direction. In those innocent days before the *Marchioness* disaster, the Birkenhead boats were allowed to carry 1,200 passengers — and frequently did. But not sufficiently frequently.

[2] The numbers are in brackets because they were not used on the boats; when Wallasey Ferries sold off boats their names were reused. The numbers are simply for historical convenience and were first made popular in Duckworth & Langmuir's *West Coast Steamers*.

The ferries, like many other municipal transport undertakings, had started life as good earners which subsidised the general-rate fund. After World War 2, both Wallasey and Birkenhead had the novel and distressing experience of seeing their ferries lose money. In Wallasey especially, the presentation of the ferry accounts provoked a fierce debate virtually every year about whether the ferries should be closed or sold off to a private operator. At one stage it got so bad that Birkenhead and Wallasey contemplated collaborating, for example by sharing the use of spare boats — but such a relationship between bitterly rival boroughs would have been going too far. There was, after all, a serious issue at stake, which was the spacing of the landing gangways: one borough would have to change its gangway spacing to match the other's — an idea not to be entertained by either party.

The continuing popularity, despite their declining use, of the ferries was an indicator of another kind of glory day. Liverpool's record tonnage of 1964 arrived in, by present standards, large numbers (namely 16,878) of smallish vessels with large crews. Most of these vessels flew the 'Red Duster' and employed British seamen, so a high proportion of Merseysiders had direct family

◀ *Guardian* at Tranmere oil depot. Ships this size were a remarkable sight in the glory days. *John Ryan*

Melo, the first 200,000-ton tanker to enter the Mersey, in 1971. *Author*

Mersey Ferries still allow you to see the ships — this is the queue to enter the Manchester Ship Canal as seen from the annual Friends of the Ferries Cruise in 1999. *John Ryan*

connections with the sea and hence an amateur interest in ship-spotting.[3] Where now a relatively small number (7,652 in 1998) of mostly very large ships use just two river entrances to the dock system which are well downstream of the city centre (plus a third in Birkenhead), in the early '60s there were another seven older entrances still in use, all of whose traffic was crossing the ferry routes. The present-day system of crude oil arriving in, typically, one large tanker per day at Tranmere was only just getting started and the old system of smaller vessels bringing in petroleum products (rather than crude) to the Dingle Jetties was still in use. In retrospect, it was all hideously inefficient, but there were lots of ships to see, and they seemed to be an indicator of prosperity. The Manchester Ship Canal was doing well, as was the relatively small railway port of Garston; all the ships headed their way went upriver, past the ferry routes. The ferry was, in short, a place to commune with one's maritime heritage.

There were other, longer-distance ferries. That to the Isle of Man was and remains mainly a matter of pleasure-trips for those outward-bound from Liverpool, not least for hordes of happy motorcylists going to the TT or the GP, who have always shown a strong sales resistance to any other route. (This is particularly true of today's rich Dutch and German leisure bikers, who get the ferry to Hull and ride to Liverpool. Heysham? *Nein, danke!*) For Manx people inward-bound it was often a matter of business or necessity. Although the IoM Steam Packet Co adopted motor vessels for its cargo services (starting with *Fenella* in 1952), it continued building smart little turbine steamers like *Manxman* (II) of 1955 for its passenger services, and anyone who, in later years, travelled one way by steam and the other way by motor would vouch for the superior quietness and smoothness of the former, even when they were getting old. New, in their glory days, they looked like toy Cunarders and, with

[3] I know this sounds like a silly joke, but the Mersey ferries are the largest vessels regularly using the port of which this is still true. The Belfast boats, for example, are registered in Limassol; the Manx boats are registered, as they always were, in Douglas and fly the Legs of Mann.

top speeds around 25 knots, went nearly as fast. They were large vessels in relation to the voyage length of around 3½ hours, carrying some 1,500 passengers in reasonable comfort — so long as the sea was not too rough. The motor vessels which replaced them used less fuel, but usually took well over 4 hours, to say nothing of sounding and smelling nasty.

Accompanying them at the Princes Stage until 1962 were the last survivors of the Liverpool & North Wales Steamship Co, sailing to Llandudno and Menai Strait. Like the Manx boats, these provided more than a pleasure-cruise: it was only partly in jest that Liverpool was known as the capital of North Wales. (Indeed, in 1900 the National *Eisteddfod* was held in Liverpool). Thursday was 'Welsh day' in the Liverpool shops, and if you lived in northwest Wales, a 19-knot steamer from Menai Strait or Llandudno was faster by far than a 60mph train to Chester, change for Rock Ferry, change for Liverpool Central, because the distance was so much less. Nevertheless, with passenger capacities up to nearly 2,500, the ferries' main traffic was for inexpensive day or weekend trips for people from Liverpool and district: Menai Strait was a good access-point for those keen on outdoor pursuits in Snowdonia (or, so I am told, indoor pursuits involving a borrowed wedding ring in The British Hotel, Bangor), while Llandudno offered the traditional attractions of the better class of holiday resort. Of course, the older passengers in the last days of the service would remember the famous and elegant paddle-steamer *La Marguerite* (1899-1925), but the turbine-steamer *St Tudno* (III) of 1926 still looked like a proper little ship. When the company went into liquidation, a partial continuation of its services was provided by the Isle of Man Steam Packet Co, which still runs a few trips, but nothing which could be called a ferry service, on the route. There is continuing speculation that Mersey Ferries might revive the service: the boats are quite sufficiently seaworthy, but their survival equipment is only of 'estuarial grade', and meeting the requirements of seagoing use would be costly.

The Wallasey Ferries' *Royal Iris* (III), of course, represented another kind of local pride. Her curvilinear superstructure rather resembled the bodywork of a mid-'50s Humber Hawk, but nothing so complimentary could be said of her colour scheme. She was designed as a dual-purpose vessel — part high-capacity ferry boat and part inshore cruise vessel. By the standards of her sisters and competitors she was huge: at 1,234 gross register tons she was nearly twice the size of the next largest ferry, and in 'ferry mode' could carry 2,500 passengers. In cruising mode she anticipated by over 30 years the role of the present Mersey Ferries, but despite her ballroom and her renowned capacity for chip-frying it was her name which was really the source of local pride. She carried the prefix 'Royal' because her predecessor, *Iris*, along with her sister, *Daffodil*, had played a significant role in the Zeebrugge raid of 1916. The raid was only partially successful in its objective of blocking Zeegrugge harbour to U-boats, but it would have failed totally had the two Mersey ferries not assisted in pushing one of the blockships into position while under heavy fire. They were given the honorary title of 'HMS' for the duration of the war, and the prefix 'Royal' at its end. In Liverpool — and more particularly in Wallasey — these things, rather than the speeches about revenue deficits, were remembered.

The Princes Stage, where these vessels plied their trade, was itself a source of considerable local pride. It had been constructed as two separate stages of which the first was completed in 1848, but in 1874 the two were united to form the longest floating structure in the world. Thanks to an incompetent gas fitter (the days of scapegoating smokers had yet to dawn) it suffered a fire as it was nearing completion, in which anything that would burn, did. It was rapidly reconstructed and fully back in service by 1876. In 1896 it was improved and strengthened to allow it to take the 'boats' of the 'North Atlantic Ferry' — Cunard's *Campania* and *Lucania*, for example. It also acquired a direct passenger rail link: the trains left the LNWR main line at Edge Hill and crept down the Victoria and Waterloo tunnels, emerging at

The Isle of Man services were always highly seasonal. Once the GP, the last big event of summer, was over, some of the boats were laid up; here we see *Manxman* and *Mona's Isle* in Morpeth Dock. *John Ryan*

The present *Lady of Mann* looks quite impressive from this angle — but in the glory days Elder Dempster's passenger liners berthed there. *Aureol* was the last in 1972. *Roy Forshaw*

▲ *St Silio*, Liverpool & North Wales Steamship Co, entered service in 1936 and was renamed *St Trillo* in 1945. Notice in the right distance the high-level gangway for passengers on the serious ships! *John Ryan*

21

From the top of the Liver Building we see modernisation at Princes Dock to provide improved accommodation for the Irish boats. But what they were starting from is not too impressive. Nor, indeed was what went before... *National Museums & Galleries on Merseyside*

... in the shape of these extremely spartan benches of 1926 vintage housed in what is effectively a small transit shed. *National Museums & Galleries on Merseyside*

Although this aerial view dates from about 1930, it gives a good idea of what the stage was like when there were still plenty of users, as well as showing Riverside station and its approaches. Notice the still-visible wake of the Wallasey luggage-boat which has just tied up: it shows some pretty expert high-speed berthing. The passenger liner is White Star's *Britannic* (III), which lived into the glory days. *National Museums & Galleries on Merseyside*

The preserved paddle-steamer *Waverley* makes occasional visits to Liverpool and conveys something of the bustle and excitement of the old floating stage. *John Ryan*

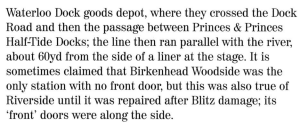

Waterloo Dock goods depot, where they crossed the Dock Road and then the passage between Princes & Princes Half-Tide Docks; the line then ran parallel with the river, about 60yd from the side of a liner at the stage. It is sometimes claimed that Birkenhead Woodside was the only station with no front door, but this was also true of Riverside until it was repaired after Blitz damage; its 'front' doors were along the side.

By the early 1960s there were no longer many ocean-going liners, though there were still a few. The stage was, however, busy with lesser vessels, and its replacement with a smaller stage, which actually occurred in 1976, would have been inconceivable. Princes Parade, the roadway which ran along the northern part of the stage, was glazed overall, in the manner of a trainshed, until one got to the bit right at the north end where the 'coastwise ferries' tied up. Coastwise passengers did not, of course, deserve or get an overall roof, and their waiting room, equipped with luxurious slatted wooden benches dating from 1926, was on the site of a former cattle pen. But they put up with it, for this was part of the heritage, in which they knew their place. They probably also had to put up with people preaching, lecturing and ringing handbells, all of which unseemly activities were banned under Bye-law at the classy end of the stage but not at theirs.

Those destined for Ireland chose the appropriate side of Princes Dock — east for Dublin and west for Belfast. These services had, in their way, been so much improved that they were quite well received. Smart, modern waiting rooms with refreshment facilities were provided, but perhaps the most striking innovation was the roll-on roll-of ramps for motor vehicles. You no longer had to drain your fuel tank and have your car or van craned aboard, and probably damaged by a cargo net. You didn't have to pay rip-off prices to refill your tank with what was almost certainly your own petrol at the other end. You just drove on and drove off. Of course if you scratched the skin you found an obsolete dock and some old sheds tarted up with plastic-faced hardboard (remember it?), but it was such an improvement on what had gone before that one was genuinely grateful.

Railways

Liverpool's trading prowess in the 19th century had made it both a leading centre for the raising of railway capital and a magnet for railway promoters. It would be quite impossible to give a history of Liverpool's railways, even if one took the whole of this book to do it, but one or two lines are deserving of special mention. Let us begin, perhaps perversely, with one which the average Liverpudlian hated: Jesse Hartley's 'Dock Line of Railway', begun in 1846 and 'completed' (though much extended later) in 1851. It ran the whole length of the Dock Road and, while by 1960 it was showing serious signs of decline, it was still possible to spend many unhappy minutes waiting on foot, on a bus or in a car or taxi while a train of 30 or 40 loose-coupled wagons passed at 2-3mph over the point at which one wished to cross its route — or where one of its numerous branches crossed the main road. A train of empty coal wagons was another matter entirely, although that traffic was dwindling, and (fortunately) a lot of it used the High-Level Coal Railway serving Bramley-Moore and Wellington Docks.

The speed was governed not by the power of the locomotive or the weight of the train, but by the flagman who was required by law to precede it on foot. There is a famous contemporary joke about a dock labourer who stamped on a snail: 'What did you do that for — it wasn't doing you any harm?' enquired his mate. 'Effin' management spy — been following me round all effin' day.' It could just as well have been told of a flagman. Yet, in a strange way, these annoyances were also a source of pride, for they were a highly visible port activity taking precedence over other forms of transport and they emphasised Liverpool's role as 'Britain's Front Door', which was the Mersey Docks & Harbour Board's advertising slogan at the time. It was all part of the old idea of being a great port — something of which people were proud even when it was a nuisance. The present

railway operations occur entirely between the Dock Estate and the main-line system: rail haulage to and from the docks is enjoying a revival. But it crosses no public roads and, like so much of the shipping it serves, is miles out from the city centre, invisible to the ordinary citizen. Ironically, it is exactly because it does not get up our noses that it is not part of the glory days.

Although the Liverpool Overhead Railway (LOR) was closed on 31 December 1956 and demolished in 1957/8, when the glory days were yet to reach their peak, it has cast a long shadow in local folk memory. It is still not hard to find people who think that it should never have been demolished, or even that we should build a new one now, for the tourists. The reality was that the railway had been built on the cheap and it scarcely ever made a profit. Its maintenance had been skimped to save money and the sum needed to repair the structure in 1956 was 80 times its net annual receipts. Looked at another way, the interest cost of borrowing the money to repair it would have been more than three times the net receipts. The company's dividends record meant that a share issue to raise new capital was out of the question because nobody in their right mind would have bought shares, and no public or quasi-public body would take it on. The idea of a new overhead is strictly for those who are away with the fairies: the Dock Road is still a busy route, but it is not busy with hundreds of thousands of people working within a short walk of either side of it. It was once rudely remarked of the Overhead's route that it went from nowhere in particular to nowhere else, and, while that was unfair at the time, it is accurate enough now.

So why did people care to the point that one could reasonably say that they *loved* it? The Overhead was a wonderful, ground-breaking project when new, but throughout living memory it had been old-fashioned, slow and uncomfortable. As I said, you can't measure glory, but here is a suggestion of one part of it. Many

LOR train 7-6-19, seen here at Seaforth & Litherland in 1955, was a most peculiar one: it had two wide-bodied motor cars and one narrow trailer and, far from being an emegency expedient, ran in this form from 1903 until closure. *T. J. Edgington / Colour-Rail IR57*

▲ With less than three months to run, a tired-looking LOR wide-bodied car No 20 leads its train into James Street station. The stock is older than the Liver Building (left background) and the White Star Line offices in the right foreground. *T. J. Edgington / Colour-Rail IR58*

Liverpudlians have always had a certain sense of 'otherness': they consider themselves different from other people, which in some respects they probably are. The charm of the Overhead was probably partly just that it was different. 'Ordinary' cities like Manchester, Birmingham or Glasgow didn't have one. Liverpool did, and that made it worth treasuring.

But if you speak to those older Liverpudlians who rode on it while it was still there, few of them mention its technical attributes, apart perhaps from its ability to run safely in quite thick fog. They certainly don't tell you how smart and fast and comfortable it was, because it wasn't. What they will mainly tell you about is the joy of riding along looking over the boundary-wall of the docks. The docks were secret places to those who did not work there, enclosed for their seven-mile length by walls which were typically about 16ft high, their gateways guarded by the Dock Police. There were a few places where you could catch a glimpse of the inside: the Dock Board had not managed to block the view from the footwalk of the Stanley swing-bridge, for example, but all you could normally see there were a few coasters in Salisbury and Collingwood and some of the Board's salvage camels in Stanley. If you were really lucky there might be an Irish cattle-boat waiting to use Clarence Graving Docks. From the railway, your view was blocked by warehouses or granaries at a few points, but nearly all the line of docks was spread out before you: ships carrying the trades of all nations, most of them flying the 'Red Duster'; passenger liners in dock taking on cargo, stores and baggage 'not wanted on voyage'; especially lucky passengers might get to see the Board's 200-ton floating crane *Mammoth* (predecessor of today's *Mersey Mammoth*) loading railway locomotives for East Africa or oil-processing equipment for Nigeria.

This is a very warped view of a fascinating experiment in urban transport which acquired a string of technological 'firsts' from the time of its opening in 1893 and was of considerable — if financially unrewarded — importance in the continuing expansion of the port. But it is what people remember, and, in so far as the Overhead is part of the glory days, this is because it, like the ferries, offered a point of contact otherwise denied, between Liverpool people, the ships and the sea, for Liverpool was and is a city of the sea. As early as 1816, HM Customs had required Princes Dock to have high perimeter-walls, and these walls spread both up and downstream to a total

This is the last of the LOR's series of posters offering views of the docks, published in the late 1930s. Top attractions for ship-spotters were the Gladstone system, with the graving dock in the right foreground, Branches 1 and 2 centre/left mid-ground and the entrance and Gladstone Dock proper beyond and to right. The floating crane exhibits some artist's licence, but is obviously intended to be *Mammoth*.
Ian Allan Library

length of about seven miles. This denial of ordinary people's access to the river remains a source of acrimony to this day, and the wish to 'see inside the walls' was a powerful one which profited the LOR. When the *Empress of Canada* caught fire in Gladstone Dock (January 1955) and capsized through a miscalculation of how much water could safely be pumped into her, the Overhead enjoyed a mini-boom carrying the voyeurs who wanted to check on how far the Dock Engineer's and Marine Surveyor's men had got in righting her. Reputedly the busiest day in the railway's history was that of the opening of Gladstone Dock in 1927, and we may be sure that the people that filled the trains were mostly not of the same class as those invited to the luncheon. The company was naturally aware of this as an advertising feature, and published a set of colour posters — the first dating from well before World War 1 — illustrating the sort of thing one could see from the railway, and accompanied by such tempting slogans as 'Affording Magnificent Panoramic Views of the Liverpool Docks'.

The Mersey Railway, touched upon in the introduction, had a distinctly inglorious early history, passing into receivership[4] within a year of opening and descending deeper into debt at an ever-increasing rate until its electrification in 1903. From then on, it provided a fast and

[4] As mentioned in the Introduction, it is worth passing note that the creditor chiefly responsible for putting the railway into receivership was the Borough of Birkenhead, which, as a major ferry operator, was not exactly disinterested.

◀ A Mersey Railway train of the second batch of Westinghouse stock, which lacked the open platforms, at Rock Ferry. Notice the four-rail system, intended to diminish earth leakage, which was abandoned when the Wirral Railway was electrified on the third-rail system. The stock lingered on. *Ian Allan Library*

Some of the last batch of Mersey Railway stock: although the open platforms have gone, the American-looking clerestory is still very prominent. This scene is at Birkenhead North in 1957, when they had not long to go. None of the stock survives, and even photographs are hard to find. *J. B. McCann / Colour-Rail DE1666*

▲

A Class 503 EMU (car M28673M leading) approaches Wallasey station on the former Wirral Railway, bound from New Brighton to Liverpool Central in 1960. *J. B. McCann / Colour-Rail DE1733*

▶▶

frequent service between Birkenhead and Liverpool, and also connected at Birkenhead Park with the Wirral Railway to West Kirby, New Brighton and Seacombe, at Rock Ferry with the LNWR/GWR Joint line to Chester and (again via the Wirral Railway) at Bidston with the MSLR line to Wrexham. Its original Westinghouse electric stock looked as though it had been acquired secondhand from the props-buyer of a cowboy film, complete with open-end platforms from which to shoot at the Birkenhead Indians. It had many teething-troubles, both structural and mechanical, but once these were sorted out it served pretty reliably into the 1950s, looking more ridiculous, as well as shabbier, with every passing year. Its punctuality, however, was legendary: it was timed to miss the connection with the 58 bus at Rock Ferry and it always did.

The Wirral line was electrified on the 650V DC third-rail system in 1938, with smart new LMS stock of all-welded-steel construction, similar to that introduced very shortly before on the Liverpool Exchange–Southport line. The clean lines of these new trains, and perhaps particularly their pneumatically-operated sliding doors, gave them a very modern image. The change at Birkenhead Park was abolished, and the new Wirral trains ran through to Liverpool Central. The heavy

The island platform at Bidston where the Wirral branch to New Brighton and the GCR route to Wrexham turned off respectively north and south. *John Ryan*

gradients of the tunnel required a high power-to-weight ratio, so the journey-time from West Kirby to Liverpool was cut from 36 to 29 minutes.

The Mersey Railway had successfully — if ill-advisedly — striven to avoid inclusion in the Grouping. It remained independent and therefore had no money for new stock. After nationalisation, services over the Wirral and Mersey routes were in theory fully integrated, but passengers on the original Mersey route, now known as the Rock Ferry line, still mostly rode on the old stock, and it was not until 1956 that the first of its 24 new trains (later designated Class 503) took to the rails. They were almost identical to

the Wirral trains, and the changeover was completed during 1957. It is hard to remember that Rock Ferry station still had six platforms — four through ones on the Woodside–Chester line (which was quadrupled in 1893) and two bay platforms for the Mersey trains — which gave a certain aura of importance to a somewhat unimportant place. The booking hall, which seemed enormous in relation to the number of people using Platforms 3 to 6 for Chester and beyond, and cramped in relation to the number wanting Platform 2 for Liverpool, was built on the overbridge. It is perhaps symptomatic of the ending of the glory days that Birkenhead Woodside closed in 1967, and

This train of Class 503 stock is in fact heading for Central, but is reversing round the junction at Bidston to avoid re-ballasting work. Bidston used to have another junction, until the Wirral route to Seacombe was closed in 1962. Both had full triangles — but only if one counts some non-electrified tracks serving the docks. *John Ryan*

A Class 503 (M28690M leading) at Birkenhead North in 1956, passing some old Mersey Rail stock which will soon be away to the breakers. *D. A. Kelso / Colour-Rail DE1885*

▲ Birkenhead Docks were rather a failure in the trades for which they were designed, but succeeded in becoming important (among other things) for bunker and export coal. This view is of the coaling plant serving the locomotives serving the coaling berths at the west end of the Great Float. *Colour-Rail DE1457*

This sums up the reduced aspirations of railways: Rock Ferry station's old booking hall above and its new one below. *John Ryan*

Before modernisation, Rock Ferry was was not exactly imposing, but it was quite spacious, and expressed a measure of self-esteem. *John Ryan*

the slow lines to from Chester were cut off at the end of the platform to allow a 'level change' from third-rail electric to diesel, leaving the fast lines for freight to and from Birkenhead Docks. This enabled the demolition of the booking hall and its bridge: they were replaced by a booking office resembling an oversize bus stop.

Never mind; Merseysiders now had smart-looking trains which were bigger and faster than those on the Glasgow or London undergrounds — the only systems with which local people saw fit to compare them. It is an interesting reflection on their travelling public that throughout the glory days, a three-car set had three quarters of a car given over to First class, and a five- or six-car set had one and a half.[5] The First class was, naturally, in the trailer cars, so that one's perusal of the financial column of *The Beano* was not disturbed by the noise of traction motors or brake pumps. While the quality of the seating was not particularly opulent, its size — three seats abreast in a carriage of very near main-line loading-gauge — was. There were occasional complaints during the '50s that the public would be better served with one-class trains, but these were repudiated by British Railways on the grounds that the two-class service was more profitable. Quite soon, the former First-class passengers would be driving their company cars to the company car-park. Non-smokers were tolerated to the extent of about a quarter of each car being enclosed for their use by a sliding door which usually stuck.

It sounds stupid to say it now, but the Mersey Railway in the '60s did actually convey the impression that one was in a very important place. Trains ran under the river on a three-minute headway, yet the platforms were always busy. The high power-to-weight ratio needed to cope with the 1-in-26 maximum gradient in the tunnel meant that at busy times a departing train normally

accelerated to over 30mph in the time it took for its length to clear the platform, creating a sense of purposefulness. Unfortunately, although what there was of it provided a good service, it had no connection with any other lines on the Liverpool side. You could, of course, climb the stairs to join the former Cheshire Lines routes from Liverpool Central High Level, but these were already running down and Central High Level eventually closed in 1972. Getting around or across Liverpool by rail, as distinct from in and out of it, remains relatively difficult today, even after the large Loop/Link investment of the mid-'70s joined the former Cheshire Lines route to Hunts Cross with the former Lancashire & Yorkshire routes to Southport, Ormskirk and Kirkby.

Part of the problem was that in the 1920s, when Unemployment Grant Commission money had been available for major urban railway projects, the Liverpool trams offered far too good a selection of routes for the local railways ever to get together to form anything of comparable quality to the London Underground. Even the proposed 'Belt Route' around the city, nearly all of which already existed as tracks of the CLC, L&YR and LOR, was not built. It was not that the railways were not there — simply that nobody turned them into what the tramways were, namely a coherent system rather than a collection of odds and sods built at different times for different purposes by different people.

It would be nice to claim that the Liverpool suburban services of the main-line railways were butchered by Dr Beeching, but it would not be true. Perhaps the darkest year was 1948, when the LNWR branch from Edge Hill through Tuebrook and down to the docks closed to passenger traffic, sweeping away several stations in densely-populated areas. The CLC route to Southport, ostensibly duplicating the L&YR but in fact reaching a number of places the latter did not, followed in 1952. The next major closure was not until 1972, when the CLC route from Hunts Cross to Walton succumbed. The only significant closures during the glory days were the stations at West Derby, Sefton Park (both 1960), Aintree Cinder Lane (1962) and Aintree Central (1963).

[5] The original intention, as well as the recent pactice, was to use two three-car sets coupled — obviously a more rational arrangement than using five-car sets. I have not found the reason for the occasional five-car sets, though it could possibly have been to release motor coaches for routine maintenance, withdrawing one coach only instead of three.

A Class 503 (M29143M leading) approaching Platform 5 at Rock Ferry on arrival from Liverpool in 1959. This view gives some impression of the spaciousness of what was, apart from its joining the former Mersey Railway with the former LNWR/GWR joint line, really a rather unimportant place. *G. H. Hunt / Colour-Rail DE2027*

It is 22 August 1968 and Liverpool has now lost its connection with the former GWR. A Park Royal DMU (still painted green) leaves Rock Ferry from Platform 1 bound for Chester General. *John Ryan*

Goods and passengers meet. To the right are the lines connecting the former CLC with Herculaneum Dock, to the left the line from Central to Hunts Cross. In the cliff above is the tunnel portal of the Southern Extension of the LOR, while not far behind the camera is the site of the former Brunswick passenger station, recently re-created for Merseyrail.
John Ryan

Continuing an old Lancashire & Yorkshire Railway practice dating back to the earliest days of electrification: parcel & baggage car M28496M at Exchange station in 1964.
C. R. Gordon Stuart / Colour-Rail DE1884

41

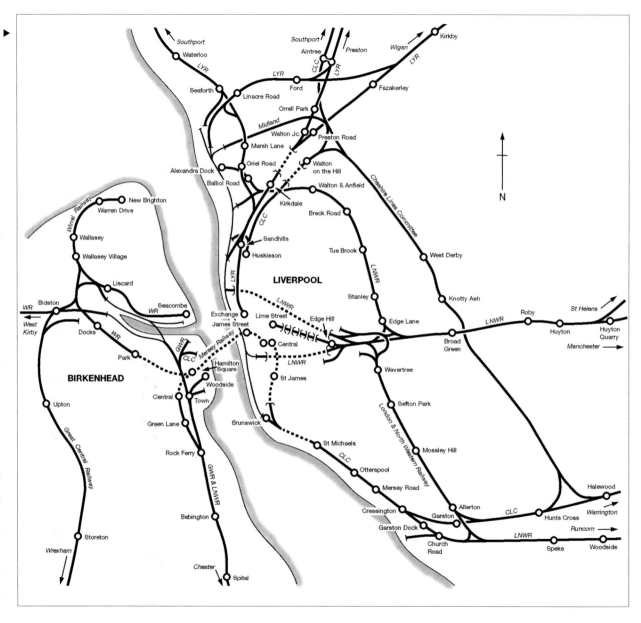

This map of the Liverpool area's railway network is of composite date to show the maximum extent of the system.

42

Garston Church Road station was on the LNWR route from their main line to Garston Docks. From here one could travel via Allerton, Mossley Hill, Sefton Park and Wavertree to Edge Hill. But not in the glory days, for the service was withdrawn in 1947. *John Ryan*

Mossley Hill is a small station on the former LNWR main line. Because Mossley Hill housed many of Liverpool's most important businessmen, it was quite important and had a slight revival in the late '60s when some University Halls of Residence were built nearby. *John Ryan*

43

This lovely old postcard shows a London express stopped at Wavertree in 1900. (The locomotives have their blowers on.) Wavertree did not live into the glory days, and if it had we may be sure that the expresses would not have stopped there. *John Ryan*

Litherland was just one of several Liverpool districts with a choice of stations: Linacre Road on the L&YR line to Ormskirk and Seaforth & Litherland on the Southport line. *John Ryan*

The L&YR's terminus at Liverpool Exchange, which did not look all that different when it closed in 1977. In the glory days this was an important station, serving nearly all the routes northwards — and many eastwards — from Liverpool. *John Ryan*

Orrell Park, perhaps surprisingly, still exists on Merseyrail's Northern Line to Ormskirk. Between Walton Junction and Sefton Junction there were eight stations on three different routes, all within a mile of each other. *John Ryan*

The L&YR had been very early (1904) in electrification, and while Bootle station (by then Bootle Oriel Road) did not look as good in the 1960s, it still enjoyed a good electric service in to Exchange and out to Southport. *John Ryan*

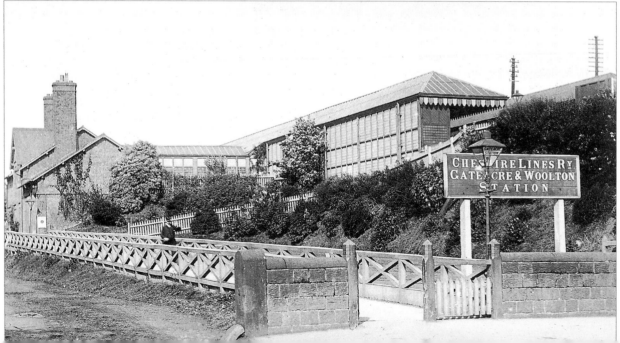

Gateacre & Woolton, later abbreviated to Gateacre, was on the CLC route from Hunts Cross to Walton, and could be reached from either Lime Street or Central (High Level). This line closed in 1972; had it instead been connected to the original Liverpool & Manchester route at Broad Green it could have taken the pressure off some of Liverpool's most congested roads. *John Ryan*

West Derby is three stops on from Gateacre. Further north, the line branched to Southport (closed 1952), Huskisson Dock (where there was briefly a passenger station) and back towards L&YR territory at Sandhills. *John Ryan*

Some people saw at the time that here was a glorious opportunity being missed. There existed the bones of an urban system to rival the linking of U-bahn and Schnellbahn systems achieved in the postwar reconstruction of major West German cities, yet it remained fragmented, needing a curve here or a junction there. A route existed, for example, from the CLC southbound from Central, via the Garston Dock branch, onto the LNWR and back to Edge Hill, and thence to the north docks via some of the most densely-populated parts of the city. The CLC 'Belt Route' crossed the LNWR a little east of Broad Green and a little south of Knotty Ash: a junction station there would have

plumbed the large and growing population of Childwall into a route to the city centre. Then it crossed the L&YR route to Ormskirk... But the sad fact is that suburban services like these needed investment and they did not get it. Like barefoot children on the step of a Victorian beer-house, they watched the glory days from the outside. The reason is simple: they were not viewed as suburban services but merely as feeders to the main-line termini.

Who were the people who saw this? One group which did — and it was by no means unique — was the Liverpool University Public Transport Society. This was a hopelessly over-ambitious group, whose finances were

Otterspool station was the only one on the CLC line south which was working during the glory days but was abandoned when the line was reopened as part of Merseyrail. It was in a very sparsely-populated area and presumably existed chiefly to serve various sports grounds which existed on land held by the railway and the Dock Board for possible future development. *John Ryan*

What is Class 40 No 40 118 doing in a dead station? St Michael's closed in 1972, but the tanker trains from Dingle oil depot carried on, and 40 118 is on its way to collect one. *John Ryan*

And here's his mate going the other way. The date is 3 June 1975, by which time the oil traffic had kept the line open long enough to allow ideas to change and for it to be electrified and reopened to passenger traffic. *John Ryan*

49

more chaotic even than those of the public transport systems it supported, but it was extraordinarily good at organising excursions. In particular, in 1964 it ran the 'Liverpool Suburban Tour', which covered 60 miles. Starting from Edge Hill, it ran down the Waterloo Tunnel to Riverside station and then along the Dock Railway to Alexandra and up to Kirkby Industrial Estate, then via Aintree & Sefton Junction to the former L&YR North Mersey Goods Depot; from there it ran to Walton on the

Hill and thence via the former CLC to Huskisson Dock. Every one of these lines had at some stage carried passengers and, it might be argued, should have done again. The reason most of these routes had closed to passengers long before the motor car offered serious competition was that nobody except the amateurs saw any need for strategic planning of transport services, and the initiative had been seized and retained by municipal electric trams.

Riverside station (closed 1972) was not exactly in its pomp in the glory days, but was still in use. This, however, is a Special organised by the Liverpool University Public Transport Society in 1966. (The locomotives are 2-6-4 tank No 42236 and 'Black Five' No 45039.) *John Ryan*

The same Special on its way back, here seen entering the ex-LNWR Waterloo Goods Yard *en route* for Edge Hill. In the '60s, as the LUPTS sought to show, there were considerable mileages of freight lines, forgotten by the public, which could have formed a proper rail network. *John Ryan*

51

No-one could say of Liverpool Central (Low Level) in its glory days that it lacked character. This view dates from 1975, just before the great facelift began. In the '60s it was a very busy place indeed, but imagine it in the days of steam working. *John Ryan*

▲

Trams

Trams were something which Liverpool did rather well, yet their greatest achievements were as the pawns of other policies of the City Council. When the first electric trams were introduced, in 1898, they had two main aims which had nothing to do with the wants or needs of the travelling public. The first was to consume a lot of electricity during hours of daylight: the Corporation had embarked on a policy of large-scale electricity generation at a time when electricity was used almost solely for lighting. It was highly desirable to find daytime uses for large amounts of electricity to spread the load around as many hours of the day as possible, and trams were an excellent way of doing this. The easiest way for them to gain traffic was not by pioneering new routes but by offering a better or cheaper service on an existing route, and the trams did severe damage to the Liverpool Overhead Railway by following this policy consistently. In terms of an overall transport policy this was insane, but at the time nobody had any idea of an overall transport policy — and it is questionable whether, a century later, we have learned from the mistakes of our ancestors.

The second main aim of the tramways was less publicly known, yet more important in the way in which the tram system developed. To John Brodie, City Engineer 1898-1926, trams were a matter not of transport but of social engineering. Liverpool had a long-standing problem of insanitary over-crowding in what we now call 'inner-city areas', to which the only answer was to allow the city to spread, to reduce population density. The trams were the tool for the job: new areas on the outskirts of the city were opened up by the building of large dual-carriageway roads with tram reservations in the centre. These were, technically, light railways; running on railway-style tracks and, isolated from other traffic, they could sustain speeds which undoubtedly exceeded the 30mph officially admitted. (Anecdotal evidence suggests that 50mph was achieved on rare occasions.) These huge roads were built on land acquired for low or even nominal prices on the

Both the trams in this view slightly pre-date the completion of the Municipal Power Stations at Lister Drive and Pumpfields. *John Ryan*

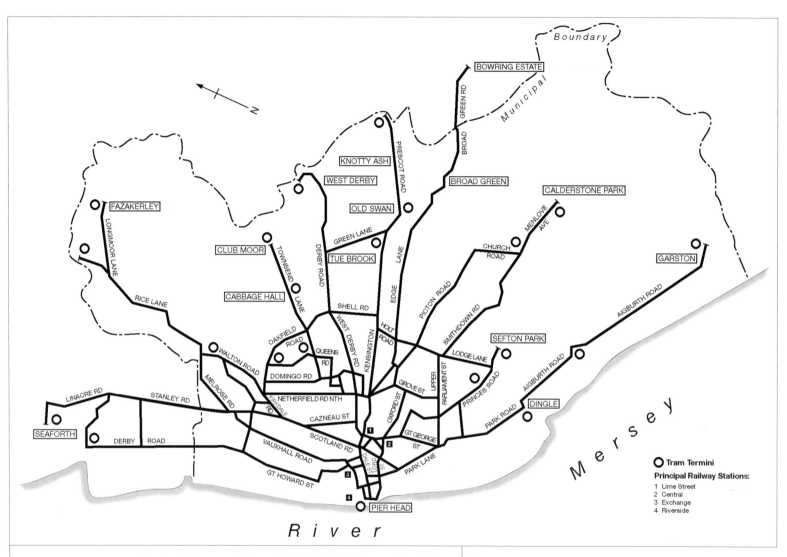

BOUNDARY

BOWRING ESTATE

Municipal

KNOTTY ASH

PRESCOT ROAD

WEST DERBY

BROAD GREEN RD

BROAD GREEN

CALDERSTONE PARK

OLD SWAN

FAZAKERLEY

MENLOVE AVE

LONGMOOR LANE

GREEN LANE

CLUB MOOR

TOWNSEND LANE

DERBY ROAD

TUE BROOK

CHURCH ROAD

GARSTON

EDGE LANE

RICE LANE

CABBAGE HALL

SHELL RD

PICTON ROAD

SEFTON PARK

OAKFIELD ROAD

WEST DERBY RD

HOLT ROAD

SMITHDOWN RD

AIGBURTH ROAD

WALTON ROAD

QUEENS RD

KENSINGTON

LODGE LANE

MELROSE RD

DOMINGO RD

UPPER PARLIAMENT ST

PRINCES ROAD

AIGBURTH ROAD

LINACRE RD

STANLEY RD

KIRKDALE RD

NETHERFIELD RD NTH

OXFORD ST

GROVE ST

PARK ROAD

DINGLE

SEAFORTH

CAZNEAU ST

DERBY ROAD

VAUXHALL ROAD

SCOTLAND RD

GT GEORGE ST

1

DALE ST

LORD ST

GT HOWARD ST

PARK LANE

3

4

M e r s e y

PIER HEAD

○ Tram Termini

Principal Railway Stations:
1 Lime Street
2 Central
3 Exchange
4 Riverside

R i v e r

The electric tramways of Liverpool in 1914, showing their connection to the
suburbs. The system was further extended between the wars, and would
remain substantially intact until the 1950s.

▲

grounds of the betterment to landowners when development spread along the new roads and their tramways. The much-vilified 'ribbon development' which followed was no accident; it was planned and enabled by Brodie. At one level, the trams allowed the working classes to move out to new housing areas; at another they allowed the middle classes to move even further out, to areas like Woolton, leaving their former residences to 'gravitate' to the upper working class. Menlove Avenue, the main tram route out to Woolton, was no less than 120ft wide.

But yer typical Scouser did not read the *Town Planning Review* (itself a Liverpool 'first', first published in 1908 by the Department of Civic Design, Liverpool University, and still going); he just thought that the streamliner trams — the four-wheelers were known as 'Baby Grands' and the eight-wheelers as 'Green Goddesses'[6] — were pretty impressive, which they still

[6] Strictly speaking, the title 'Green Goddess' is not specific to the streamliners, but refers to any Liverpool eight-wheeler, of which several designs entered service before the streamliners appeared. It has, however, been popularly applied only to the streamliners.

◀ 'Baby Grand' tram 258 stands at Pier Head, where there were connections with ferries to Birkenhead and Wallasey.
Roy Brook

were when the last one ran in 1957. There were, of course, still some older cars around in the '50s in which it was a favourite schoolboy amusement to shear the end off a pencil by inserting it in the gap that appeared between the window-glass and the frame when accelerating and disappeared when braking. But, as we always say in justification of things which are well-loved despite being demonstrably inadequate, they had *character*.

The reality of the matter was that the tramways, like so much else, had emerged from World War 2 with woefully obsolete stock in a state of grievous arrears of maintenance. Furthermore, they emerged into a climate of shortage of key materials and of skilled labour. The extreme example was the survival of 'Bellamy'-type car 544, built in 1910, which continued in service until 1949. At the same time as this was going on, the Overhead Railway seemed somehow to be able to get sheet aluminium, other bodybuilding materials and the labour to use them for building its 'modernised stock' — between 1945 and 1947 it turned out six completely-rebodied carriages, which was no mean achievement for such a small undertaking. (Though it might merely mean it had friends in the right places.)

In the immediate postwar years, the Corporation's policy was to acquire more buses, even if second-hand

'Baby Grand' 293 carrying out ceremonial duties on 14 September 1957; as at the closure of the Liverpool Overhead Railway, large and emotional crowds gathered. The conversion to buses had been going on in the background, and by this time there were only 30 cars left in service. *Ian Allan Library*

58

from other operators, to get some sort of service running again quickly, and it was not until the early '50s that the disgraceful queue of trams awaiting attention in the works — which at times amounted to 25% of the fleet — began to dwindle. It is possible, of course, that the nationalisation of electricity generation played a part here, given the close connection which had always existed between municipal power generation and tramway consumption. Perhaps trams had suddenly become less important.

Trams had always been built down to a price and a weight, and often exhibited basic engineering weaknesses like having their bodies hog or their platforms droop. Of course, engineers could have built flawless tramcars, as Frederick Royce built (almost) flawless motor cars, but they would not have been affordable. One design weakness of the Baby Grands was that they had wire resistances for controlling their traction motors enclosed in a cupboard under the stairs, where they could overheat through lack of ventilation, occasionally actually catching fire. It was one of these Baby Grands, the last new Liverpool tram design, which was responsible for Liverpool's own *Göttertrammerung* in the shape of the Green Lane depot fire of 1947, which destroyed over 10% of the total stock, much of it the best and most modern in the fleet. Put another way, over 13% of the *operational*

◀ This really was the end: 293, bringing up the tail of a procession of 13 cars, enters Edge Lane Works.
Ian Allan Library

59

'Baby Grand' 245 was kept for eventual preservation by what was then the City of Liverpool Museums. The Museum had no suitable premises even for quality storage, much less display, and the expedients adopted to avoid this problem caused some ill-feeling from time to time. Here she is being loaded at Edge Lane Works to travel to one of her temporary homes. *John Ryan*

stock was lost. Of course, if the poles had been de-wired overnight, the accident could not have happened, but then the cleaners could not have turned on the cars' interior lights in order to do their duty. But there was a rumour that cleaners were in the habit of tampering with controllers so as to provide themselves with a little local heating from the resistances. The author has no personal experience of tram controls, but has driven a pre-World War 1 electric crane in which just such things were possible.

And what did we think of the trams when they had gone? We loved them, because the ones we remembered were the good ones, which were smoother, quieter and more comfortable than buses. They were much bigger, too. We forgot the crazy situation which had applied before about 1950 when there were so many clapped-out old ruins on the system that the high-powered bogie cars were crawling along, reduced to the speed of the slowest car on their line — and that was SLOW. On some of the substitute bus services, prewar AEC Regents achieved

significant reductions in journey time, which should have been out of the question when the streamliners could accelerate at 2mph per second — a considerably brisker rate than that of a small family car of, say, 1948. An ageing Regent I could, with luck, do 0-30mph before lunch.[7] But the trams, especially the streamliners, had a certain magic about them — and because of Liverpool Corporation Transport's long-term policy of in-house construction there was nothing exactly like them elsewhere. In the Scouse Glory Days Dictionary of Synonyms, 'different' meant 'inferior', or, more colloquially, 'under de arm'.

[7] It was about 1962 that I came to read the Owner's Manual for a 1932 Model Y (8hp) Ford, which proudly claimed that it was possible to accelerate from 0 to 30 mph in under half a minute, but then conceded that this involved the use of 'racing gearchange techniques' which the ordinary driver might be unable to master. The rude remarks about Regents do not, of course, apply to new ones: the 1949 Regent III could do 0-30 in 17.2sec, but it had the 9.6-litre engine which gave about 30% more horsepower than the 6.5-litre engine of the Regent I, supported by an apparently bottomless pit full of torque.

◄ The same occasion viewed from the other end. The good news is that, despite her travels, she still survives in eminently restorable condition.
John Ryan

Buses

Because Liverpool went in for trams in a very big way and at an early date, enthusiasm for the early motorbus was very limited. While the Fire Service could experiment with internal combustion, purchasing its first Daimler motor appliance (which rapidly acquired the nickname 'Farting Annie') in 1904, Liverpool's first attempts at a motorbus service waited until 1911. The famously rapid development in lorry construction forced on by the Great War resulted in no great bus construction programme in Liverpool, and what buses were bought came from a wide variety of manufacturers. Some attempt was made at standardisation in the late '20s, in the shape of a fleet of six-wheeler Karrier and Thornycroft chassis which were bodied, mostly as single-deckers (though some of the Karriers were fitted with truly monstrous double-deck bodies), in-house. The timing was not good: these vehicles were designed to allow buses large enough to compete with trams to comply with legal limitations on axle loading. A slackening of these restrictions in 1930 turned all the six-wheelers into cumbersome over-engineered dinosaurs and none remained in service more than seven years.

The Thornycroft, for example, used the WD-type four-wheel-drive fully-articulated bogie designed for 6x4 military transports, mounted 'upside down' with its driveshafts under- instead of over-slung to achieve an acceptably-low floor-height. For its intended job it was a good bogie; under the back of a bus it was unnecessary, complex, heavy and expensive.

Throughout the '30s, Liverpool trams made profits which buses consumed — or so it appeared at the time. A more sophisticated analysis might have shown the buses as a valuable feeder to the tram services, but the figures which were gathered do not reveal this, for they were not intended to. They were intended to protect the tramways' investment in permanent way, the Corporation's

investment in generating plant, its income from the rates on tramway installations and the noticeable contribution to highway maintenance made by the tramways. It may well be significant that in Birkenhead, which bought its tramway electricity from Liverpool, tramway abandonment was complete by 1939. From the start, tramway and power-generation finances had been closely linked.

Liverpool pretended to take the bus/tram controversy seriously, but in reality it was not until the immediate prewar years that specialist bus depots began to appear, or, more importantly, that any attempt was made to build a rational fleet of buses based on large orders of few types. The first AEC Regents entered service in 1935, and further orders followed at an increasing rate until 1940, by which time 172 buses — all basically the same for maintenance purposes — formed a significant proportion of the fleet.

The war years were, naturally, characterised by buying whatever was available, usually in small orders, but by 1946 Regent IIs were fairly readily available and 100 were bought by 1948, closely followed by 100 Regent IIIs. Leyland Titan PD2s now made an appearance, which would be consolidated with some large orders between 1952 and 1955, and down to the end of the trams the bulk of bus orders was for variants of the Regent or the Titan. These were competent modern buses, and reputedly were well received, but they were not obviously different to the average traveller from what had gone before. To Joe Public, one Regent looked much like another. There might be a bit of 'Merseypride' in the fact that the buses were better than they used to be, but there was no 'hinge-point' or break with tradition. They had open rear platforms and half cabs, and they spent a lot of time in workshops having their springs re-bushed through running on roads with setts and tramlines. A bit of pride, perhaps, but scarcely glory.

Just imagine meeting this monster in the daytime fog! The first of 18 AEC Regent IIIs delivered in 1953/4 with unpainted aluminium bodywork by Saunders-Roe. *Lancashire Press Agency / Ian Allan Library*

▲

▲ Experience with the invisible aluminium buses led to their gaining a green band, as seen here in 1964 on L308, a 1961 Leyland PD2 with Crossley/MCW body. In the background are the Cunard Building to the left and the Dock Offices to the right. *Geoff Lumb*

In the early '60s Liverpool was able to make large investments in public transport; this is the new Gillmoss depot of 1962, to the east of the city. *Ian Allan Library*

▲

▲ The main workshop at Gillmoss depot, shortly after opening. *Ian Allan Library*

Speke, another outlying area with a growing population, no railway station and a lack of local shops, had its new depot, not quite of the size of Gillmoss, in 1957. *Ian Allan Library* ▶

This Leyland Titan PD2/30 had a 1960 chassis but was newly into service when this shot was taken on 4 March 1962. It is believed to have been the last new half-cab bus to enter service with LCPT. *John Ryan* ▶

Weymann-bodied Leyland PD2 No L21 passing Lime Street station. The Royal Hotel and its neighbours were demolished to make way for a small row of shops and a high-rise office block, but the North Western Hotel — largely derelict, with parts being used as temporary offices by British Railways, throughout the glory days — is now restored as student residences for Liverpool John Moores University. *Geoff Lumb* ▶▶

The Liverpool Show used to be a major event: here is part of LCPT's display in 1958, featuring a Regent chassis and a number of components. Interesting though it is, it seems rather a departmental ego-trip and by 1970 the ego was completely deflated. *Ian Allan Library*

In the glory days, it was possible to do something about abnormally-long bus queues: four of these radio-equipped Morris 1000 Travellers cruised their respective divisions and could summon extra buses to a particular route if necessary. (Radio control was first introduced in 1954, but this particular vehicle is a 1958 model.) *Ian Allan Library*

Glory came with two developments: the experimental Leyland Royal Tiger one-man single-decker and, more particularly, the Leyland Atlantean double-decker. The Royal Tigers seemed to hold out the promise of smart and efficient feeder services on the minor routes. They were arguably Liverpool's first single-deckers to look anywhere near as stylish as contemporary private coaches, but there were not many of them, and they served few routes. It may be that they were an idea ahead of their time — but we know what happens to ideas like that. The successful ideas are ideas *of* their time.

The really visible change was the introduction of the Atlantean. It is often said of the London Routemaster that it was the first bus which was actually designed as a bus rather than being a converted lorry with a low floor and seats. It was a pretty radical vehicle, employing independent front suspension and a chassisless monocoque structure. It was arguably the most successful bus design of all time and quite large numbers are still giving good service now when over 40 years of age; they have become a design icon. Yet it might be equally true to say that the Atlantean was the first service double-decker which *visibly* owed virtually nothing to lorry design. The Routemaster disposed its major mechanical elements as in a forward-control lorry, with the driver sitting alongside an engine which had a gearbox behind it and a long propshaft to a conventional rear axle. It had its front wheels virtually at the corners and a substantial

overhang behind its rear axle. Perhaps significantly, it continued to waste a significant cubic footage of its 'envelope' at its front nearside corner. Despite its radical design and its numerous detail refinements, in basic configuration it did not look fundamentally different from a 1935 Regent.

The Atlantean did: its overhung transverse rear engine and transmission made it resemble a Regent or a Titan as much as a Hillman Imp resembled a prewar Minx, and we must remember it first appeared in 1956. This was, to borrow a BMC (remember them?) slogan, 'creative engineering'. Here was a bus which, thanks to recent changes in regulations[8], could at last carry nearly as many people as a tram, could look as smart as the streamliner trams and have power-operated doors like they did. Maybe they were initally a bit short on horsepower — they used the same 125bhp engine as the Titan — but their automatic clutches coupled with pneumatically-controlled Wilson-type pre-selector gearboxes gave them quite impressive acceleration in the dense traffic in which they mostly operated.

[8] The maximum permitted width was increased from 7ft 6in to 8ft in 1946, and length from 30ft to 36ft in 1961.

Route 1, the service which was supposed to replace the Overhead Railway, on the Dock Road, with Cunard and Liver buildings behind. The bus, E2, is the experimental Leyland Atlantean/ MCW whose success led to large orders. Later in the glory days, the Luftwaffe-designed car park in the foreground would be occupied by Wilberforce House, one of the worst of Liverpool's '60s buildings, now rendered palatable by heavy post-modern restyling. *Leyland Motors/ Ian Allan Library*

The facility with which they changed down, ready to hit peak torque out of the corner, was perhaps more important than their slick change up. In the decade in which modernism ruled supreme, here was a modern bus, and Liverpool ordered 200 of them in 1961. Of course the direct-injection AECs made a nicer noise, especially those which were fitted with the superb 9.6-litre engine, which could hit its governor while travelling fully laden up the side of a house. But who, outside the Liverpool University Public Transport Society, cared about that? The Atlanteans took up the baton from the streamliner trams: they re-established Liverpool as a place where one could be proud of public transport.

As I write this, I can hear the cries of 'Rubbish!' in sitting-rooms from Inverness to Penzance. In a sense, they are right, for the Atlanteans were in some ways less satisfactory than the Regents and Titans they replaced. Yet the main failing of the Atlantean was a comparatively minor one: the structure of the rear outriggers which supported the engine covers; modified more than once, they still failed to defy Sir Isaac Newton and Daniel Higson alike, and drooped hideously. But we are not here to argue about that; we are concerned with the public perception of the new Atlanteans when the first 200 appeared on the streets. That perception (wrongly, for there were all manner of old rattlers still on the road) was of a completely new and modern bus fleet, and it was one which Liverpool had never enjoyed before.

Brand-new Leyland Atlantean/MCW L501 of 1962, giving a good view of the engine bustle characteristic of the type. This feature later gave minor but frequent problems due to drooping — not a desperate matter, but it ruined the fit of the panels, giving the whole vehicle a very unkempt appearance.
Liverpool Corporation/
Ian Allan Library

Leyland Atlantean/MCW L545 standing at the top of South Castle Street in June 1963, with Derby Square in the background. The trams have been gone for years, but their memory lingers on, especially for cyclists. Northwood, shown on the destination blind, is one of the districts of Kirkby. Today the street has disappeared under the forecourt of the Queen Elizabeth II Law Courts. *J. A. Upton Woods*

By 1966, when L754 was new, it was easy to find scenes like this showing four recent Atlanteans and not a half-cab in sight, even if two of them are being (as Flanders and Swann put it) 'very gregarious' by travelling the same route in tandem. But the picture also shows the lamentable failure of Liverpool's reconstruction in the '60s, with clearance of 'unfit' property merging seamlessly with reamaining Blitz damage, tramlines still in place and street lights still suspended from the remains of the traction supply. *T. W. Moore*

The second batch of Atlanteans (Mk IIs) had a much sleeker appearance, mostly resulting from the improved proportioning of the upper and lower windows. L759, with L796 in the background, approaches Pier Head on 21 May 1966.
John Ryan

LCPT and its successors made a number of attempts at providing services like the City Circle, generally with only limited success. This was particularly surprising when L164 (an Alexander-bodied Leyland PD2 of 1953) posed for the camera in 1965, as Liverpool still had three main-line termini, one of which (Exchange) was badly placed for the shopping centre. That centre, too, was more diffuse before the spread of high-density shopping developments like St John's Precinct.
Liverpool Corporation / Ian Allan Library

◄ Notice the number 14c in centre frame. It is an Alexander-bodied PD2/20, seen here in Clayton Square in 1969. Careful scrutiny reveals a non-standard stanchion under the nearside corner of the upper deck, reputedly put in as a temporary measure following accident damage in 1955. *John Ryan*

◄ One of the 1956 Leyland Royal Tigers in its reincarnation as an airport coach (XL171), seen outward-bound on Park Road in May 1970. *Geoff Lumb*

One-man operation might be taken as a symptom of the end of the glory days; be that as it may, it returned with these Metro-Cammell-bodied Leyland Panthers, introduced in 1968. *Ian Allan Library*

Among the last buses delivered to LCPT before its absorption into Mersyside PTE in 1969, 1120 was one of the so-called 'Jumbo' Atlanteans, with an Alexander body on a long-wheelbase chassis. The scene is South Castle Street, with bomb-site car parking still evident. But at least in the glory days the driver and the conductor could enjoy a cigarette together before pulling out. (You may need your magnifying glass.) *M. R. Montano*

A sad state for an AEC Regal, adapted as a staff canteen — but a sadder comment on the self-image of LCPT in its last days. *Ian Allan Library*

In the glory days, however, it was possible to have smart purpose-built canteens. This Bedford-Scammell dates from 1948. *Ian Allan Library*

Illustrations from an article in the 17 April 1936 issue of *The Electric Railway, Bus and Tram Journal* entitled 'Modernising Liverpool's Transport', showing (top right) car body building, and (bottom left) the paint shop. The smaller pictures, top to bottom, show the sawmill, the sheet metal department, the blacksmith's shop, and the machine shop, showing the newly installed wheel lathe in the foreground. *The Electric Railway, Bus and Tram Journal*

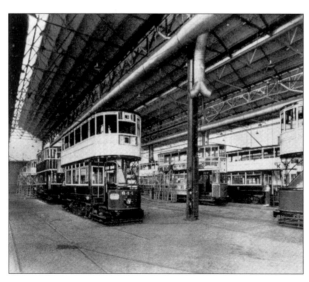

In retrospect it must be conceded that, while Atlanteans may have had their problems, the later deliveries (to Merseyside PTE) lasted in service until late 2000, running at perhaps twice their intended economic life and suggesting that the popular perception of them was less than totally wrong. It is certainly open to question whether any subsequent Liverpool bus has introduced as many new design features at one stroke, but the impact of the Atlantean was followed up by the extremely smart-looking Leyland Panther and Bristol RE single-deckers which introduced one-man-operation on minor routes.

While the image of the Passenger Transport Department was mainly influenced by its vehicles, there are other factors to consider. Time-keeping was always fairly erratic, and frequently exhibited the legendarily infuriating phenomenon of there being six buses once an hour instead of the advertised one every 10 minutes. This, however, was a problem in every large city, its universality perhaps confirmed by its incorporation into a characteristically-splendid comic song by Michael Flanders and Donald Swann. Where the Department let itself down badly was in the standard of some of its 'installations'. Canteens for drivers were made out of old bus bodies and left in highly-visible positions, including the car park at the back of the Municipal Buildings. In at least one case, a complete bus was used, and the problem of the local hooligans stealing it in the middle

This view, taken during the glory days (1966), shows three ancient relics together at Edge Lane Works. The oldest of them is A522, an AEC Regent II dating from 1947 and presumably awaiting disposal, as its destination blinds have been removed.
Ian Allan Library

A529 was a Regent III bodied at Edge Lane Works on Weymann frames in 1948. It is seen outside the Mersey Mission to Seamen, waiting to turn right into James Street. In the foreground, the Dock Railway is still in place (and in use), and the tram lines down to Mann Island have still to disappear under tarmac. This is, believe it or not, 1966.
Geoff Lumb

of the night was solved by dumping a cubic yard or two of readymix on the site and then backing the rear wheels into it and leaving it to set. These filthy eyesores were perpetrated by a local authority which would go to a good deal of trouble to stop 'gypsies' parking up on derelict land in Everton.

There was one very notable exception to this policy of making do. Just as some of the stable buildings of the predecessor horse-tram companies had pretended to some style, so the Edge Lane Works of the Liverpool Corporation Passenger Transport Department was among the largest in the country and sought to project a dignified image. Although it dated back to 1924 (begun — completed 1926), in the glory days it was still a most impressive edifice, with a 200yd-long grand frontage in a vaguely Renaissance style with Portland stone enhancements and a squat but substantial clock-tower. It was designed to build and maintain large quantities of trams in a fully-integrated manner; contracting-out of specialist aspects of the work does not seem to have been considered. But the reason for this was one which has a certain modern resonance — namely that the Corporation preferred to spend its money on employing local people. So the works contained its own smithy, pattern shop and foundry and sawmill, in addition to extensive bodybuilding and repair, overhauling and paint shops. It had main-line railway access at the rear for deliveries of the raw materials of tram-building, of petrol (initially, diesel fuel later) for the buses and fuel for the boilerhouse. Also at the rear was a separate building for dealing with bus repairs.

Round the sides and the back, the architectural prettying-up vanished, but the sheer size of the place and the comprehensive nature of its facilities could not fail to impress. It contained over three miles of tram track, of which two miles were indoors — and 'indoors' amounted to 7¾ acres. It may well have been a *folie de grandeur* from the start, but even in the '60s, when its original mission of building tram bodies was over and it was under-employed, it was still a most imposing building. By then, anyone who understood these things knew that

huge integrated facilities of this kind were collapsing under their own weight and administrative complexity, but of course few people did understand that, and accepted it as another tenet of the creed of pride in Liverpool transport. The skids had been put under it before the war: the first purchases of Regents had also been the first purchases of complete buses rather than chassis to be bodied at Edge Lane, as the six-wheelers had been. Some of the new buses ordered in the immediate prewar years were either chassis-only or chassis with Weymann frames for construction or completion at Edge Lane. A pretence was still kept up in the '60s by making a few in-house mods to the Atlanteans, but the Baby Grands were in fact the last new product to emerge from Edge Lane entirely built on the premises.

By the late '60s, Edge Lane, having performed well in the tram reconstruction programme immediately after the war and the subsequent major thrust on conversion to buses, was living off scraps. A workshop designed as a manufacturing facility was reduced to making some pretence at earning its keep by such means as maintaining the two civic Rolls-Royces, which it understandably did extremely badly, resulting in a series of scandal stories in the local press.

Another building which was briefly a source of some admiration was the new bus terminus at Pier Head. Once the famous three tram circles had gone, it was possible to park the buses herringbone-style at bays, making best use of the space available and minimising the need for passengers to encounter the often unpleasant weather at the Pier Head. A long, covered walk connected the bays, and was provided with a concourse area, refreshment facilities, lavatories, shops and an information office. Completed in 1965, it had an elevated 'promenade deck' for watching the river on nice days and a pleasant first-floor restaurant for enjoying the same view in worse weather or better company.

Put like that, it sounds pretty good. In fact, the project had been envisaged since the end of the war and had been subject to almost endless delays as a result of the

PIER HEAD, LIVERPOOL.

▲

This view of Pier Head is taken from the top of the Dock offices c1950. Riverside station has been rebuilt, but the three tram circles have not yet been reduced to two. Notice the segregation of buses from trams, and that neither extremity of the floating stage is visible.
John Ryan

involvement of a multiplicity of public bodies all wanting their say. The problems began with overlapping interests in different committees of the City Council, continued with the long-winded involvement of Central Government, and rambled yet further because some of the land required belonged to the Mersey Docks & Harbour Board. While all this went on, the facilities provided for travellers were those which had been inadequate and outdated in 1939; the only change was that in 1939 they had last been painted within living memory. By 1963, when the new development finally got underway, they probably had not.

I remember it opening, and it seemed a tremendous improvement. It was probably the 15 or so years' anticipation which made it seem so good. Quentin Hughes, however, unkindly wrote of it in 1969 that the buildings 'seem frail and temporary, an unfortunate impression largely dictated by the choice of the wrong building materials'. Professor Hughes was wrong: the impression was not unfortunate; it was exactly correct. Ill-seasoned softwood, badly painted and used in conjunction with aluminium extrusions, would have ensured a short life in Pier Head's wind-borne salt spray even had it been adequately maintained, which it was not. By the mid-'80s, when Liverpool was about at the trough of its economic problems, this building had become a disgrace even by the low standards then prevalent. Its depressing character, created partly by the fact that nobody ever cleaned the windows, was probably a factor in the declining numbers of travellers on both buses and ferries. Like a benefits office built in the '60s, it conveyed the impression that no-one would go there from choice.

1953 Leyland PD2/Weymann No L24 is beginning to look a bit dated, surrounded as it is by shiny new Leyland Panthers and Bristol REs, with Atlanteans in the background. This 1969 view also gives an impression of what was good about the new bus station — its layout. *Geoff Lumb*

PIERHEAD

Bars & Restaurant

But like much else in the '60s, it conveyed an air of modernity and progress which was convincing at the time, and we liked it, even if not for long.

The folly of it all comes over quite nicely in planning documents of the day. The 1952 Development Plan expounded the merits of the new Central Bus Station which was to be built roughly where the present one actually is. But this was not to be any common-or-garden Bus Station: this one was to have a heliport, another of the technological marvels of the age, on its roof. Writing as one who has often wished for a 20mm cannon to shoot down the Police helicopter when it flies over my house making a God-awful noise in the middle of the night, I wonder how well people would have liked the noise of constant comings and goings in the city centre? After all, nobody had even suggested that completely-silent nuclear-powered helicopters were just around the corner. An even more fundamental failing was the assumption that passengers of the class which could afford to travel by helicopter would wish to walk down a failed escalator into a dark concrete bus station where the smell of the hamburger barrow competed with the smell of diesel fuel. (Have you ever wondered why amateur bus preservationists can keep the vital fluids inside their vehicles, but professional bus operators can't?) You do not need hindsight to see that these people were sadly deluded.

The demolition of the 'new' Pier Head Bus Station in 1996 was the major local improvement of the year.

Other Buses

There were two other operators working in and out of Liverpool during the glory days. Crosville Motor Services, established in Chester as early as 1911, operated southwards to such alluring destinations as Widnes and Prescot: these are places where the people speak with a different accent, marking them out in Scouse terminology as 'woollybacks'. The replacement in 1961 of the old Widnes[9] transporter bridge with the present bowstring bridge allowed through services from Liverpool to Chester, from where there were routes extending all over North and Mid Wales. This was not, however, a happy period for Crosville's Welsh services: large numbers of them were cut completely in 1966, and the company concentrated on the areas of greatest population density.

The Crosville fleet may have been of interest to bus enthusiasts because of the company's different purchasing policy, particularly its choice of an almost 100% Bristol fleet. There was the odd Bedford here or there, but the company bought a total of 593 Lodekkas over the years, making it by far the largest customer for the model.[10] But surely these services and the buses

providing them were part of the glory days only if you lived in Widnes. Let us get this quite clear: during the glory days, if you lived in Widnes you claimed that you lived 'just outside Liverpool'. In fact, the Crosville fleet had a good reputation for cleanliness, maintenance and time-keeping which enabled it to be very much a part of the glory days: just as the North Wales Steamship Co had done, it bonded an outlying area to Liverpool as a 'central place' to which people went for their shopping or entertainment. Conversely, it provided easy access for Liverpool Rugby League enthusiasts (because, contrary to popular belief, some Liverpudlians were and are capable of appreciating sports other than football) to support the famous old teams in Widnes, Warrington and St Helens.

The Lodekka was a great improvement on its predecessors, because Crosville had hitherto used lowbridge bodies in the interests of interchangeability between routes. These had a sunken aisle at one side and a huge step up to the quadruple seats. After ascending this step no normal person could stand up straight to get to or from their seat. They were great fun for brawling schoolboys and an absolute pain for everyone else. The Lodekka's cranked rear axle allowed the lowering of the floor of the lower deck, allowing a flat-floored upper deck with central aisle. But the fact was that it was still an old-fashioned bus with its driver in a box and a big hole at the front nearside corner, even when it got a front entrance with power-operated doors. Later, when the glory days were past, the adherence to Lodekkas caused a great deal of ill feeling because they were not suitable for conversion to one-man operation.

Crosville DLG792, seen standing at Mann Island in July 1956, was a 1955 Bristol LD6G bodied by ECW. The building immediately behind it is the Mersey (road) Tunnel ventilator, and in the background the Overhead Railway is still in business. The handsome vista to India Buildings in the right background was once again due to Blitz damage! *G. Mead*

[9] Yes, I do know that everybody called it 'the Runcorn transporter', but everybody was wrong, as the terracotta legend on the (surviving) office building of the Widnes Transporter Bridge Co shows.

[10] The second-biggest was Bristol Omnibus Co, with a mere 481.

Crosville No DFB149, a coach-seated Bristol FLF6B with ECW bodywork, stands in Hamilton Street, Birkenhead, ready to set out for Caernarvon in May 1970. At around 80 miles, this was quite a long way to travel by double-decker. *Geoff Lumb*

Crosville DFG248, an ECW-bodied Bristol FLF6G of 1968, stands at Mann Island, next to the Dock Offices, destined for Chester. This route became usable only after construction of the 'new' Runcorn Bridge: the transporter was unsuitable for buses, and the Mersey Tunnel was embargoed to them by a clause inserted in its Act for the protection of the Mersey Railway. *Geoff Lumb*

They still double-park in Mann Island to this day! The offender here is another of the coach-seated Bristol FLF6B with ECW bodywork, standing as usual outside the Dock Offices. When this shot was taken in 1963, this was in fact a rather busy road, carrying, in addition to Crosville's traffic, LCPT buses inwards for Pier Head and the Scammell Scarabs from British Road Services' depot on the sight of the infilled Manchester Dock. *M. Doggett*

Crosville Bristol LS6G/ECW No SUG292 (acquired from United Welsh) ready to leave for Heswall — one of a number of routes Crosville operated on the west side of the Wirral. In the background of this May 1969 shot is the Woodside terminus of the former Birkenhead Corporation trams and buses. *Geoff Lumb*

Bootle and sundry other townships to the north were a different matter. Around the turn of the century, Liverpool was operating 'big municipal government' on a grand scale, swallowing up outlying townships and boroughs. The only valuable one (for much of the northern part of the Dock Estate was within its boundaries) which sucessfully resisted was Bootle. But Bootle wisely decided that it was not going to attempt to run its own passenger transport service. A number of Liverpool bus and tram routes operated within, and indeed right through, the borough, but in the glory days much of Bootle was served by the red buses of Ribble Motor Services. They were rather less conspicuous than Crosville, because the Crosville buses ran into Pier Head, alongside the Dock Offices, whereas Ribble had a depot in Skelhorne Street,

to the side of Lime Street station and, coming in from the north, most of its buses did not need to pass through the busiest parts of the city centre to get there. Just a handful of its routes went to and from North John Street or Pier Head.

Ribble buses were rather smart: designed for longer average journeys than the Liverpool Corporation buses, they tended to have better seating and platform doors. The downside was that, like older Crosville buses, they often featured the dreadful low-profile arrangement on the upper deck. There were, in fact, no overbridges on the routes in and out of Liverpool low enough to require this arrangement, which seems to have been adopted purely in the interests of standardisation, allowing buses to be shifted freely from one depot to another.

◄ The exact location of Ribble 2595, a 1948 all-Leyland PD2, has not been pinpointed, but it is clearly somewhere in Litherland, with the Southport line in the background and the Rimrose Valley beyond.
Ian Allan Library

Like Crosville, Ribble buses had to use the streets adjoining Pier Head as a terminus. Here a Leyland PD2/MCW, 1481, photographed in May 1969, stands near the bottom of Water Street by the side of the Liver Building. Its destination, Netherton, is a rather drab overspill district about 8 miles northeast of the city centre. *Geoff Lumb*

A Ribble Leyland PD3/
Burlingham of 1957 stands at
Old Haymarket, with Liverpool
Museum in the background and
St John's Gardens to the right.
Arnold Richardson/Photobus

Ribble was an early and avid
supporter of the Leyland
Atlantean. This 1959 example
had MCW bodywork of similar
style to Liverpool Corporation's
E2, illustrated on page 73.
Arnold Richardson/Photobus

In several places in this book it has been suggested that a spirit of improvement was in the air, and that it did not always produce schemes which lived up to their promise, or, indeed, get implemented at all. But that was not what mattered — there have always been failures and what made the schemes of the '60s so attractive was that people believed in them. A classic example of the thinking occurs in an article written by Professor J. A. Proudlove for the *Journal of the University of Liverpool Engineering Society*, a publication which presents a curious mixture of accounts of student booze-ups with articles on the serious business the engineering students would soon be entering. Under the title 'Liverpool Rebuilds' we find advocation of 'comprehensive renewal' — demolishing and replacing buildings in blocks of several acres at a time. The reason for this was the need to keep up with 'the increased attractiveness of the city centre for the large region which depends on Liverpool for many of its services, a population which is now about 1½ million but which is expected to grow to over two millions within 20 years.'

Other experts were, however, toiling to de-centralise the city by massive clearance programs paralleled by equally-huge investment in new housing far outside the city boundaries. As the nature of what may best be termed totalitarian architecture of the late '60s became clear, the attractions of the city centre waned rapidly, and Liverpool's role as a central place was rapidly diminished as satellite shopping and entertainment centres stepped in to fill the void. In the process, the need for public transport in and out of Liverpool began to diminish, and continued to do so until very recently.

Yet again, though, the glory days were in the perception, not the reality. The idea of segregating vehicular traffic (at ground level) from pedestrians on a system of high-level walkways made Liverpool seem the city of the future. The bits which were built were an unsightly disaster and the scheme resulted in the lasting idiocy that, to get into the underground station at Moorfields, one has first to climb to the level of the non-existent high-level walkway; there is no ground-level entrance. But we didn't know that then; indeed, not many of us were even up to the trick the architects used of displaying artist's impressions in which the sun shone from the most favourable angle, even if that happened to be due north.

Another of the bright ideas they had was a motorway-standard inner ring-road. This, if built, would have exhibited all the disadvantages of walled cities, but the really fundamental error was the failure to recognise the beginnings of a trend which would soon damage town and city centres — and the public transport serving them — very seriously. It was the aboliton of retail price maintenance in 1964 which started it all: when prices were fixed, firms competed on service, but when prices could be cut they competed on price and service was forgotten. Specifically, time-limited offers combined with a reduction in free delivery services to start a trend later consolidated by the arrival of the hatchback motorcar and the credit card. No longer did one decide exactly what one wanted and order it from a store which delivered it to one's home: now one decided roughly what was wanted and went out and bought it and took it home then and there. It was the birth of out-of-town shopping, and, although it took some years to reach maturity, the critical developments all happened well within the glory days. A weakened city centre weakened public transport, and *vice versa*.

So were they really Glory Days?

So much was wrong with public transport in Liverpool in the 1950s and '60s, and so much can be seen in retrospect to have been beginning to go wrong, that it might be suggested that these were not glory days at all. Certainly the seeds of serious decline can be found, but, pursuing the botanical metaphor, it is worth remembering that a banana is not worth eating until its skin starts to go brown. The skin of Liverpool public transport, like that in many other cities, was beginning to go brown, but that was the best time to savour it. At few, if any, other times did it offer the choice of so many different routes, modes and vehicle types. Perhaps above all it offered the strange experience, probably now peculiar to the Lisbon tram system, of standing at a stop and not knowing whether what turns up next will be ultra-modern or a refugee from the Museum. Few things can give such a glow of satisfaction as the welding of a well-loved heritage with a confident view of the future, and that, despite its numerous and varied problems, was what Liverpool public transport achieved during its glory days.

The Transport Act, 1968, establishing the Merseyside Passenger Transport Executive, should have seen the start of great improvements. It offered scope for cutting out duplication of effort, for co-ordinating different modes of transport and for eliminating the silly rivalries which arose between local authorities. There were real gains and improvements, and it is highly probable that, without the PTE, we would have lost the ferries. Yet, in retrospect, it seems likely that the main result of the changes was merely a slower rate of deterioration than would otherwise have been the case. Perhaps, ironically, the Transport Act marked the end of the glory days of transport in Liverpool.

◄ We must end where we began, with the river, as an inward-bound Isle of Man boat swings round to stem the incoming tide and tie up at what was still the longest floating structure in the world. *John Ryan*